INVESTIGATING
AGRICULTURAL WASTE
CLARA MACCARALD

Wonder Books
An Imprint of The Child's World®
childsworld.com

Published by The Child's World®
800-599-READ • www.childsworld.com

Copyright © 2023 by The Child's World®
All rights reserved. No part of this book may be reproduced or utilized in any form or by any means without written permission from the publisher.

Photography Credits
Photographs ©: Alessio Orru/Shutterstock Images, cover, 2; Thierry Eidenweil/Shutterstock Images, 5; Shutterstock Images, 6, 15, 21, 22, 31; Roman Melnyk/Shutterstock Images, 9; Red Line Editorial, 11; iStockphoto, 12; Maximillian Cabinet/Shutterstock Images, 17; Harauski Yauheni/Shutterstock Images, 19; Ivan River/Shutterstock Images, 25; Jennifer Larsen Morrow/Shutterstock Images, 26; Abo Photography/Shutterstock Images, 27; Julie Deshaies/Shutterstock Images, 29

ISBN Information
9781503858077 (Reinforced Library Binding)
9781503860063 (Portable Document Format)
9781503861428 (Online Multi-user eBook)
9781503862784 (Electronic Publication)

LCCN 2021952392

Printed in the United States of America

ABOUT THE AUTHOR

Clara MacCarald is a freelance writer with a master's degree in ecology and natural resources. When not parenting her daughter, she spends her time writing nonfiction books for kids.

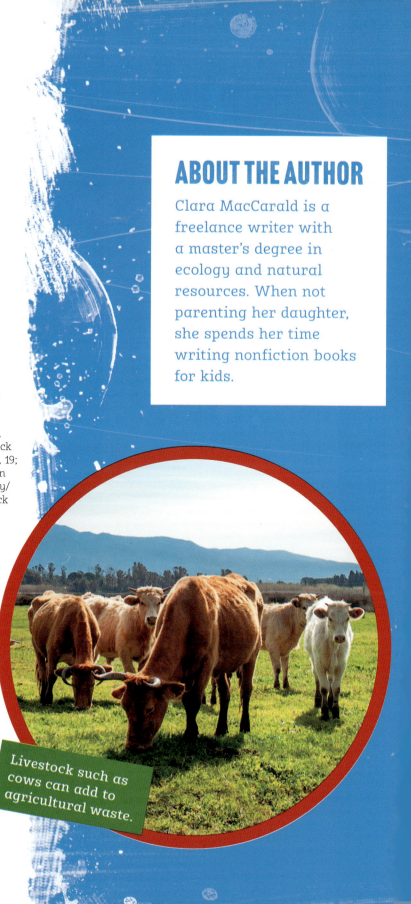

Livestock such as cows can add to agricultural waste.

CHAPTER ONE
A MANATEE IN TROUBLE ... 4

CHAPTER TWO
HARMING ANIMALS ... 9

CHAPTER THREE
POLLUTION FROM FIELDS ... 14

CHAPTER FOUR
OTHER SOURCES OF AGRICULTURAL POLLUTION ... 19

CHAPTER FIVE
TACKLING AGRICULTURAL WASTE ... 24

Fast Facts ... 28
Growing Your Own Sweet Potato ... 29
Glossary ... 30
Ways You Can Help ... 31
Find Out More ... 32
Index ... 32

A MANATEE IN TROUBLE

On April 30, 2021, a manatee named Gerard was in trouble. He lay on a beach in Palm Coast, Florida. The sun beat down on him. The three-year-old animal could barely move. He weighed only 491 pounds (223 kg). He should have been much heavier. Gerard was starving to death.

Fortunately, people discovered the sick manatee. Someone called for help. Kind strangers covered Gerard's hot body with wet towels. Soon, rescuers arrived.

Manatees are affected by agricultural waste polluting the water.

Sea turtles rely on seagrasses for their meals.

When moving manatees, rescuers usually use a special truck. The air is cool inside the vehicle. People spray water on the manatees to keep their skin moist. The rescuers moved Gerard to the truck and drove him to the Jacksonville Zoo. The zoo had animal doctors who could help him.

Not all manatees are as lucky. More than 1,000 manatees died in Florida in 2021.

Many were also starving because they could not find enough seagrasses to eat. Scientists thought **pollution** from **agriculture** was one of the causes.

> ### RED TIDES
> Large amounts of a special kind of algae create a red tide. Red tides are very poisonous. They can make animals sick or even kill them. For hundreds of years, red tides have grown off of Florida's coasts. But nutrients from agricultural pollution can make the red tides worse by feeding the algae. Red tides poisoned some of the manatees that died or were rescued in 2021.

Seagrasses once grew widely in nearby waterways. However, the waterways became more and more polluted. For years, water flowed from farms and houses into the sea. The water brought high amounts of nutrients, which are things that help plants grow. But too many nutrients make **algae** grow out of control. The algae block sunlight, which underwater plants need to survive.

Over half of the seagrass meadows near where Gerard was found have disappeared.

At the zoo, animal doctors examined Gerard and gave him medicine. Soon, Gerard felt well enough to eat. He slowly gained back his fat and his strength.

On July 14, a crowd gathered at the seashore. A truck pulled up with Gerard inside. Now, the healthy manatee weighed 605 pounds (274 kg). A team of people lowered Gerard into the water. The watchers cheered as he slipped under the waves. Hopefully, Gerard would find enough to eat in a new area. But the issue of pollution remained.

Agricultural waste is unwanted waste made when people grow crops or raise livestock. Pollution from agricultural waste can harm many living things, not just manatees. People in Florida and around the world are taking steps to tackle the problem.

CHAPTER TWO

HARMING ANIMALS

Livestock are animals raised on farms for human use. Many farmers raise different kinds of livestock. Along with common animals such as cows and chickens, some farms have rarer animals such as bison.

Farmers may raise livestock for their meat. Farms may also produce milk, eggs, or wool.

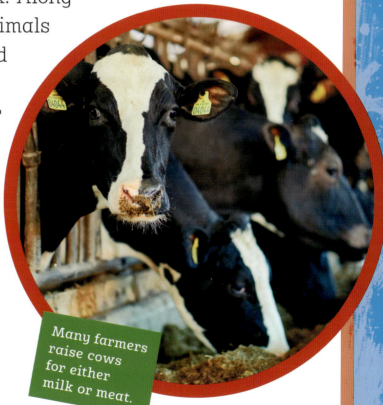

Many farmers raise cows for either milk or meat.

All of these products are things that many people eat or use.

Livestock adds to the warming of Earth by polluting the air with **greenhouse gases**. First, animals such as cows and sheep eat plants. Bacteria inside the animals' stomachs help break down the food. As the bacteria work, they produce greenhouse gases. Livestock let these gases out into the air.

Greenhouse gases trap heat on Earth. In normal amounts, the gases themselves are not bad. Without them, Earth would be much colder. Many things could not live on a cold planet. The problem is that human actions have increased the amount of greenhouse gases. And raising livestock for meat and dairy gives off about 14 percent or more of the total gases added to the atmosphere every year by people. The change is causing Earth to warm more than it should.

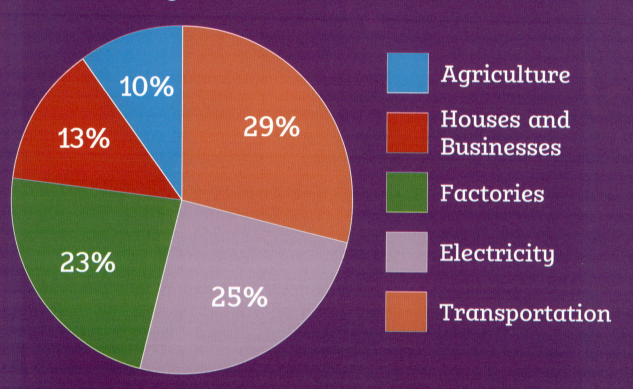

In 2019, greenhouse gases in the United States came from different places.

Manure lagoons can be lined with plastic or concrete. This helps create a wall between the soil and the manure.

A warming Earth leads to a changing climate. Heat waves are becoming worse. Arctic ice is melting, and sea levels are rising. Some areas are getting too much rain, while other areas get too little. As temperatures increase, so will certain problems. Animals that are sensitive to temperatures, like polar bears and snow leopards, may soon die out.

Livestock do not pollute only the air. They also pollute the water and soil. A problem with having a lot of livestock is that there is too much animal **manure**. Farms need to do something with all that waste. Large animal farms sometimes store the manure in large pits. These are called manure lagoons.

Along with manure and liquid waste, the lagoon's content can include chemicals, leftover medicine, and bacteria.

If farmers are not careful, manure lagoons can spill or leak into large bodies of water. This can cause a lot of problems. Because manure is high in nutrients, it can feed algae. The polluted water can kill water animals or change how they grow. Also, people or animals might drink the polluted water. Bacteria from the waste can cause sickness or death in people.

Some of the pollution from raising livestock comes from growing their food. About a third of the calories from crops around the world go to animals. One hundred calories of grain produce only three calories of beef. That means cows, for example, feed fewer people than the grain itself would. More land must be farmed to make enough food. But this can also add to agricultural waste.

CHAPTER THREE
POLLUTION FROM FIELDS

Farmers grow crops for several different reasons. Some crops feed people or livestock. Others, like cotton, end up in products such as clothes.

To give crops nutrients, farmers add fertilizers to the soil or on top of leaves to help plants grow. Farmers can use chemical fertilizers. Or farmers might add manure, which is also full of nutrients. Other chemicals farmers use are called **pesticides**. Pesticides control pests that destroy crops. The pesticides might be aimed at weeds, insects, or animals. The chemicals may kill a pest or make it leave the crops alone.

On bigger farms, people use tractors to spray pesticides.

Fertilizers and pesticides do not always stay put. They can drift away to areas outside the farm. Also, rain can wash fertilizers and pesticides into the surrounding areas. The chemicals then end up in groundwater or in bodies of water such as rivers and lakes. This water can harm animals and people.

Nutrients from fertilizers can feed algae. Too much algae can cause several different problems. As well as blocking sunlight, algae can create dead zones.

When large numbers of algae die, bacteria eat the algae. The bacteria use up a lot of oxygen in the water. But fish and water plants need oxygen to live. With little oxygen left, many things die in the dead zone. In addition, some kinds of algae make toxic chemicals that poison living things.

Too much algae is bad for plants and animals that live in the water.

Pesticides can also poison people and animals. There are hundreds of different kinds of pesticides. The chemicals work because they are toxic or unpleasant to some living things. Pesticides can kill helpful insects along with the pests.

Some insects damage crops. But many others benefit farms and people. For example, many insects, such as bees and butterflies, are pollinators. Pollinators drink the plants' nectar, which is sweet liquid created by the flowers of plants. Then the pollinators carry pollen from one flower to another. Plants need this movement of pollen to make seeds. But if pesticides are used on the plants or near the pollinators' homes, many pollinators will be killed. This means there will be fewer crops and less fruit.

POLLINATOR LOSS

Insects are not the only pollinators. Birds and bats pollinate crops and plants, too. Without pollinators, more than 100 types of crops cannot produce food. But some pollinators are dying. Pesticides poison many pollinators. Human actions have also destroyed pollinator habitats and spread diseases. Scientists are looking for ways for farmers and others to help.

CHAPTER FOUR

OTHER SOURCES OF AGRICULTURAL POLLUTION

Many parts of farming cause agricultural waste. Fields can create pollution even when the crops are gone. Bare fields are open to wind and rain, which can wash away soil. Soil that is washed away can end up filling and blocking streams. Farm soil can carry fertilizers, pesticides, and bacteria.

Erosion is when the soil slowly wears away. Bare fields can cause erosion.

Tractors on fields and trucks on dirt roads kick up clouds of dust. People and animals breathe the dust in. Breathing in a lot of dust is bad for the lungs. It can cause allergies. Smaller dust particles can even create serious health problems or make breathing problems worse.

In addition, many tractors and trucks run by burning fossil fuels. Fossil fuels are formed from the remains of ancient plants and animals. The use of fossil fuels gives off greenhouse gases.

THE DUST BOWL

In the early 1900s, farmers flocked to cheap land in the southern plains of the United States. The deep roots of native grasses held the dirt together. But farmers plowed these grasses to plant crops. They also raised livestock that destroyed the grasses and created bare fields. Strong winds tore up the soil. Huge dust storms lasted for days and blew soil as far away as New York City. People called this the Dust Bowl. The dust caused deadly breathing problems and made millions of people flee their homes.

Farms use lots of plastic. Plastic sheets protect crops. Plastic pots grow seedlings. Plastic tubes send water to fields. All of that can end up left behind in the soil or thrown out in the trash. Some types of plastic give off greenhouse gases. All plastic can break down into very tiny pieces. Small creatures in the water eat these tiny pieces. The bits of plastic can reduce their growth.

Plastic can be used to increase plant growth. But after the plants are harvested, the plastic is thrown away.

Farmers can burn parts of their fields to help plants that are about to grow. But these fires can be destructive to people's health.

   Some farmers burn plastic to get rid of it. Plastic smoke is toxic and can cause serious health problems. Some farmers burn other things on a farm, too. They can burn stems left in a field or branches cut from fruit trees. Fires remove the unwanted plant matter. Burning a field also kills weeds or other pests.

But smoke from any source bothers people's eyes and lungs. Like dust in the air, smoke can make heart and lung problems worse.

Lots of agriculture waste is created during the time between the field and a plate full of dinner. About a third of food ends up as waste. Not all crops are harvested. Some foods do not sell at the store. Some food rots. And sometimes good food is thrown away after a person has eaten his or her fill.

People might burn some of this waste. Some food might end up in the trash, such as orange peels and coffee grounds. Food that goes into the garbage can give off greenhouse gases. Also, when food is not eaten, all the pollution created to grow it is unnecessary. Farmers did not need to produce that food.

CHAPTER FIVE

TACKLING AGRICULTURAL WASTE

Farmers try to reduce agricultural waste in many ways. One thing some farmers do to help is to make their farms organic. Organic farms make an effort to improve soil, crops, and animal health without using human-made chemicals. Instead, organic farmers use mostly natural fertilizers and pest control methods. For example, leaves and other plant waste can be used as compost. Compost is rotted matter that can act as fertilizer.

There are farmers who use less fertilizer and pesticides. They use what is needed only when it is needed. For example, corn does not need a lot of nutrients to grow at first.

Using drones can help farmers reduce agricultural waste.

Spraying too much fertilizer at that time is wasteful. Later, the corn will take in a lot more nutrients. More fertilizer can go on the fields at that point.

Technology also helps reduce agricultural waste. Some farmers use small flying machines called drones to check on different parts of their fields. The machines can look for the crops that need help. A farmer can spray chemicals near those plants instead of on the whole field.

Some farmers plant cover crops to avoid bare fields. Cover crops usually do not end up on the market. Farmers can plow the cover crops into the ground when they are done growing. The plant matter adds nutrients back to the soil.

Trees and grasses planted at the edges of fields can help clean water as it flows off a farm. Farmers can also handle manure carefully by covering up loads of manure. This helps keep toxic gases from escaping. Some farmers give careful attention to the level of the liquid and solid mix in a manure lagoon. Otherwise, rain might cause the manure mix to spill out of the lagoon.

Some vineyards use crimson clover as a cover crop.

There are many ways to use food waste instead of sending it to the trash. Livestock can eat things people do not want, such as fruit peels. Some food remains become compost. People sometimes produce fuel or other products from food waste.

    The public has an important part to play. People can give unwanted (but still good) food to food banks. Food banks feed families who are hungry. Also, people can support local and organic farms by buying fresh food at farmers markets. They can compost scraps rather than putting food waste in the trash. People can also try growing vegetables or fruits at home. Agricultural pollution is a big problem, but many people are helping to tackle it.

Farmers can give chickens leftover food scraps to eat.

FAST FACTS

- Agricultural waste can pollute the air, land, and water.

- Livestock and their manure give off greenhouse gases.

- Human activities have increased greenhouse gases in the air, which is causing Earth to warm.

- Fertilizers and pesticides can run off fields and end up in bodies of water.

- Too many nutrients in bodies of water can cause algae to take over. Algae can sicken or kill living things.

- Pesticides can harm crops. Also, the chemicals may kill helpful species such as pollinators.

- Organic farmers use natural fertilizers and natural pest control.

- Some farmers reduce pollution by using fertilizers and pesticides only when and where they are needed.

- People can help tackle agricultural waste by not wasting food.

GROWING YOUR OWN SWEET POTATO

MATERIALS
- ☐ Clear jar
- ☐ Water
- ☐ Toothpicks
- ☐ Sweet potato
- ☐ Knife

DIRECTIONS

1. Ask an adult to help cut a sweet potato in half.

2. Fill the jar with water.

3. Insert four toothpicks around the middle of the halved sweet potato.

4. Put your sweet potato into the jar. Make sure that half of the sweet potato is in the water and the other half is above. The toothpicks should be holding your sweet potato in place.

5. Place your jar near a window with a lot of sun.

6. Check on your sweet potato every day. Make sure the water level stays the same. Also, change out the water to keep it fresh.

7. After four weeks, you should start to see roots and sprouts on your sweet potato. You can then take the sprouts and plant them in dirt.

GLOSSARY

agriculture (AG-ri-kuhl-chur) Agriculture is the raising of crops or animals. Agriculture feeds people around the world.

algae (AL-jee) Algae are tiny plants or plantlike organisms with no roots or stems. It is a problem when too many algae grow in bodies of water.

greenhouse gases (GREEN-howss GAS-ez) Greenhouse gases are gases that trap the sun's heat. Too many greenhouse gases are bad for the environment.

manure (muh-NOOR) Manure is animal waste that can be used as a fertilizer. Farmers can help their crops by applying manure to fields.

pesticides (PES-ti-sides) Pesticides are chemicals that kill or hurt pests. Farmers apply pesticides to clear weeds.

pollution (puh-LOO-shuhn) Pollution is something harmful that is added to the air, land, or water. Farmers can do many things to reduce pollution coming from their farms.

WAYS YOU CAN HELP

- Take your extra food to a food bank.
- Reduce food waste by putting only food you will eat on your plate.
- Ask your family if you can start a compost pile.
- Talk to your family about buying organic food when possible.

FIND OUT MORE

In the Library

Carmichael, L. E. *How Can We Reduce Agricultural Pollution?* Minneapolis, MN: Lerner, 2016.

Martin, Claudia. *Food Warrior.* Minneapolis, MN: Bearport Publishing, 2021.

Rooney, Anne. *Agricultural Engineering and Feeding the Future.* New York, NY: Crabtree Publishing, 2016.

On the Web

Visit our website for links about investigating agricultural waste: **childsworld.com/links**

Note to Parents, Teachers, and Librarians: We routinely verify our Web links to make sure they are safe and active sites. So encourage your readers to check them out!

INDEX

algae, 7, 13, 16

cover crops, 26

food waste, 23, 27

greenhouse gases, 10, 11, 20, 21, 23

manatee, 4–8
manure, 12–13, 14, 26

organic, 24, 27

pesticides, 14–17, 18, 19, 24
plastic, 21–22
pollinators, 18